MONTREAL PHOTOS BOOK 2

BY S. E. MCKENZIE

Copyright © 2019 S. E. McKenzie
All rights reserved.
ISBN-13: 978-1-77281-062-2

DEDICATION
To everyone who would like to lose themselves in the splendor of Montreal.

CONTENTS

CONTENTS 1
SIGHT SEEING 3
MONREAL COMPLÉMENT CIRQUE 2019-1 4
NOTRE DAME DE LOURDES CHAPEL-1 5
JAZZ FESTIVAL 2019-1 6
JAZZ FESTIVAL 2019-1 7
PLAGE DE L'HORLAGE 1 8
PLAGE DE L'HORLAGE 2 9
PLAGE DE L'HORLAGE 3 10
PLAGE DE L'HORLAGE 4 11
CLOCK TOWER 1 12
CLOCK TOWER 2 13
L'INTERNATIONAL DES FEUX LOTO-QUEBEC 2018 14
JAZZ FESTIVAL 2018 15
GRAND ORGAN FESTIVAL 1 16
GRAND ORGAN FESTIVAL 2 17
WORLD TRADE CENTRE 18
CRESCENT STREET FESTIVAL 2019-1 19
CRESCENT STREET FESTIVAL 2019-2 20
NOTRE DAME DE LOURDES CHAPEL-2 23
NOTRE DAME DE LOURDES CHAPEL-3 24
VILLAGE-1 25
JUST FOR LAUGHS PARADE 2018-1 27
JUST FOR LAUGHS PARADE 2018-2 28
JUST FOR LAUGHS 2019-1 29

JUST FOR LAUGHS 2019-2	30
JUST FOR LAUGHS 2019-3	31
JUST FOR LAUGHS 2019-4	32
JUST FOR LAUGHS 2019-5	33
CONSTRUCTION 1	34
CONSTRUCTION 2	35
GOING BACK IN TIME 1	36
GOING BACK IN TIME 2	37
OLD PORT 1	39
OLD PORT 2	40
OLD PORT 3	41
OLD PORT 4	42
JAZZ FESTIVAL 2019-4	43

MONTREAL Photos Book 2

SIGHT SEEING

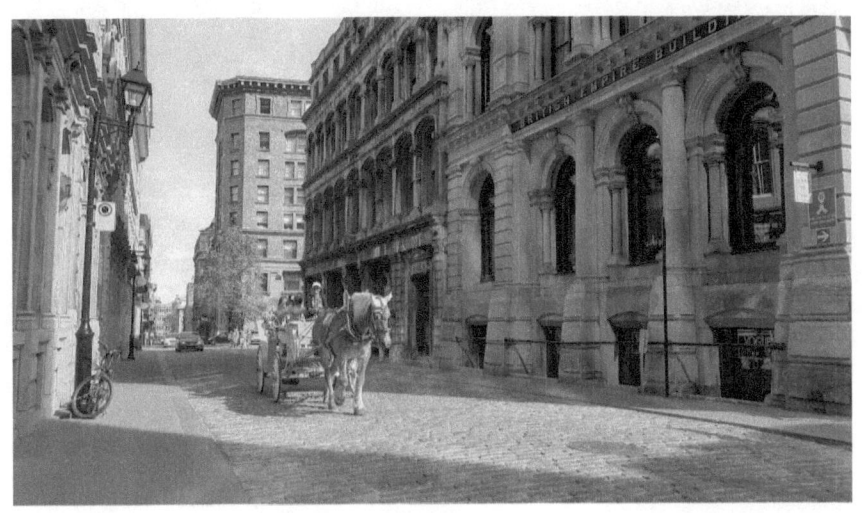

S.E. McKENZIE

MONREAL COMPLÉMENT CIRQUE 2019-1

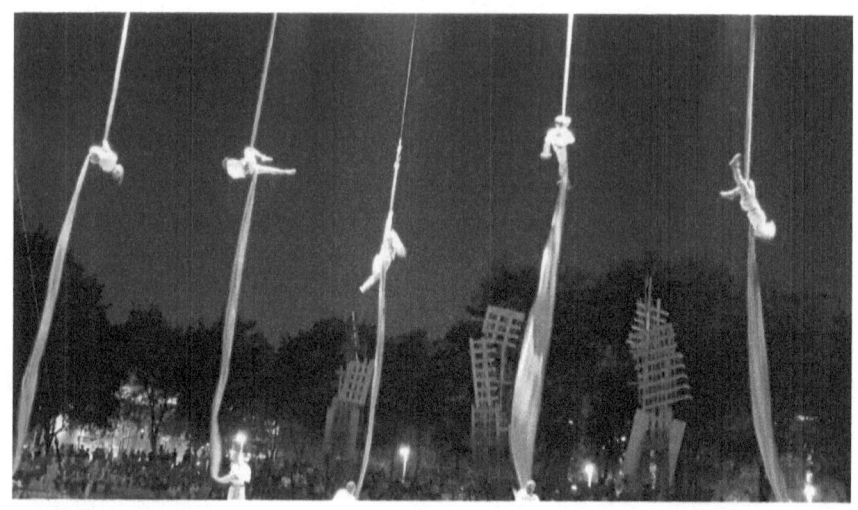

MONTREAL Photos Book 2

NOTRE DAME DE LOURDES CHAPEL-1

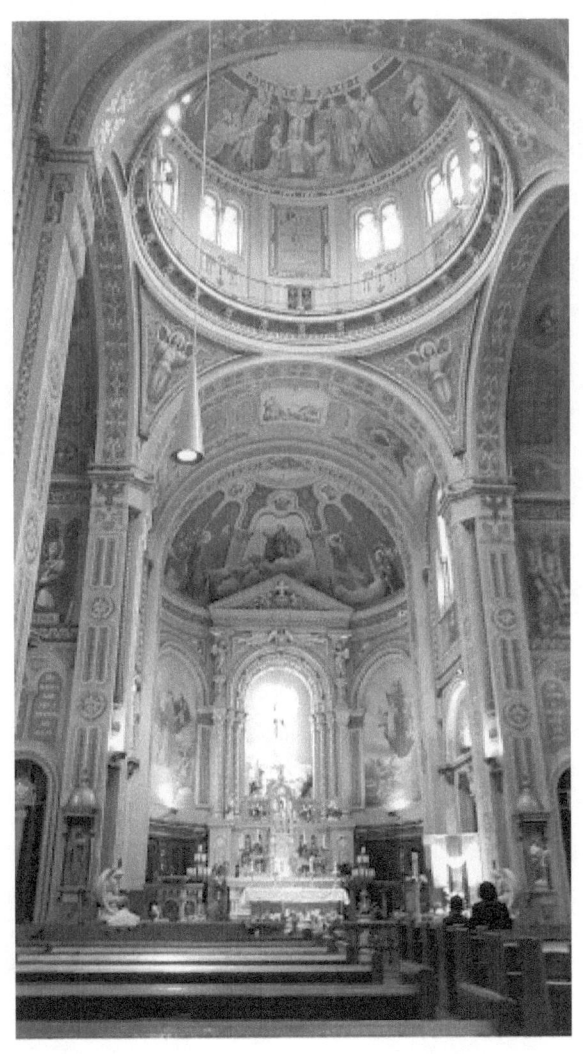

S.E. McKENZIE

JAZZ FESTIVAL 2019-1

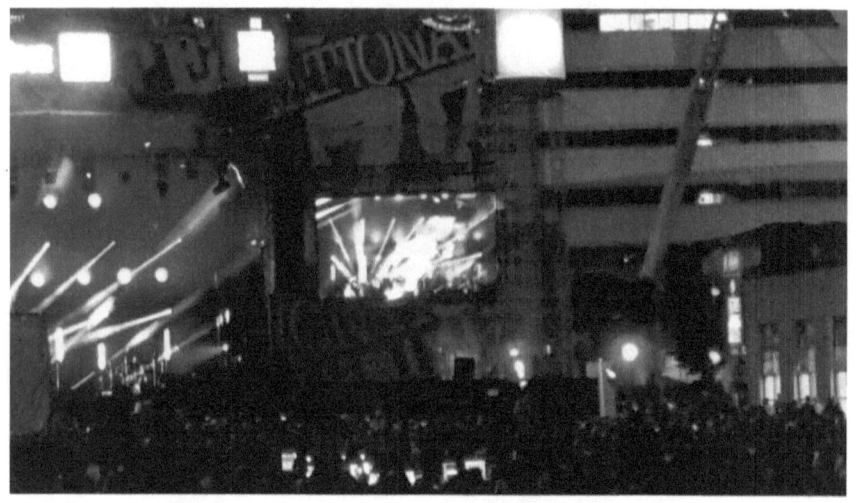

MONTREAL Photos Book 2

JAZZ FESTIVAL 2019-1

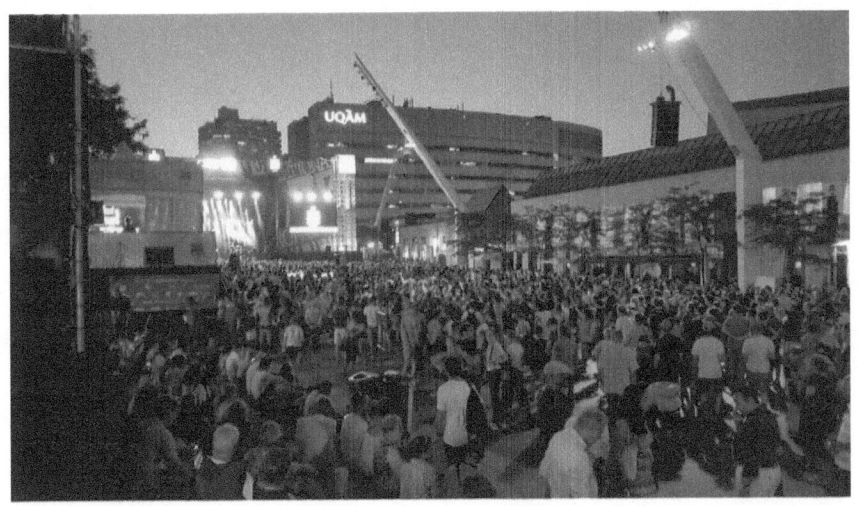

S.E. McKENZIE

PLAGE DE L'HORLAGE 1

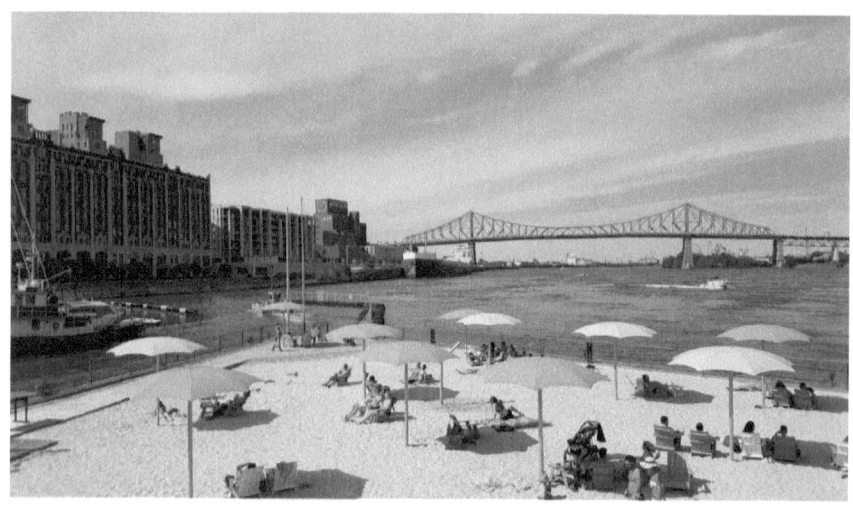

MONTREAL Photos Book 2

PLAGE DE L'HORLAGE 2

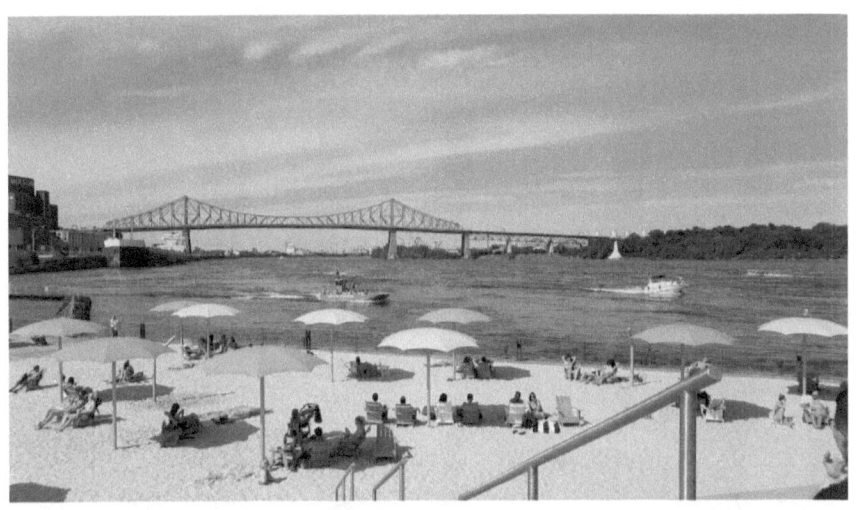

S.E. McKENZIE

PLAGE DE L'HORLAGE 3

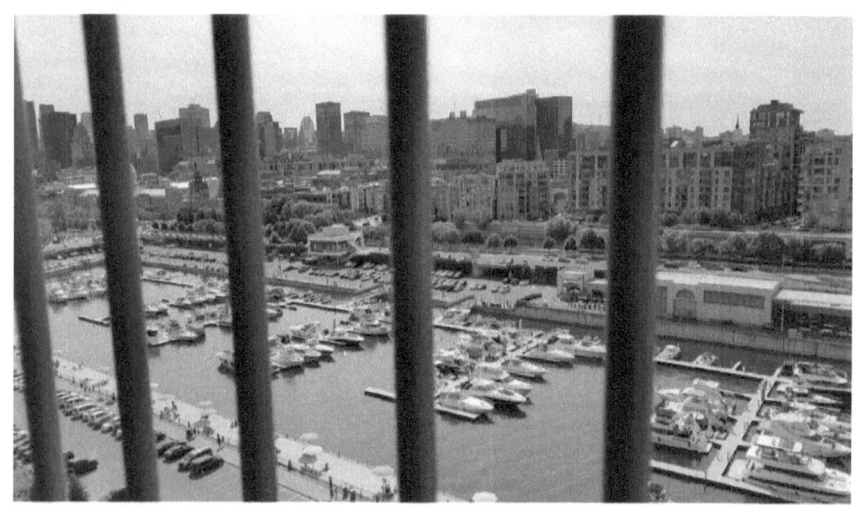

MONTREAL Photos Book 2

PLAGE DE L'HORLAGE 4

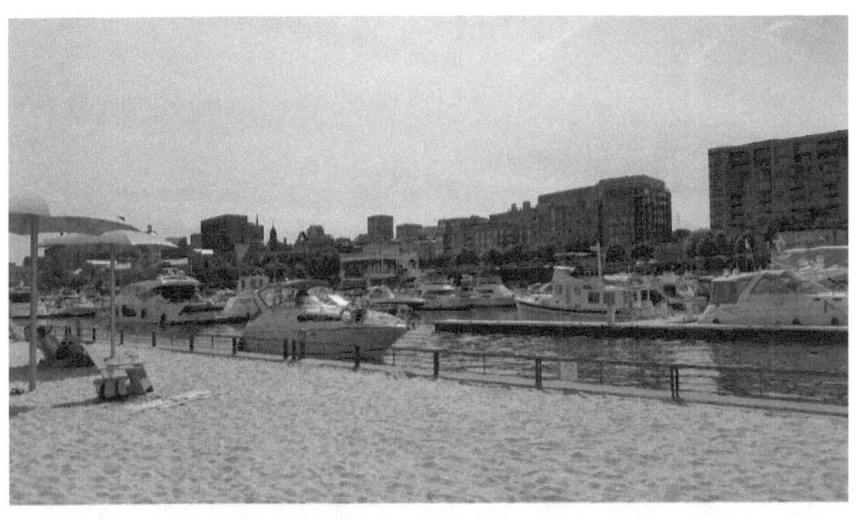

S.E. McKenzie

CLOCK TOWER 1

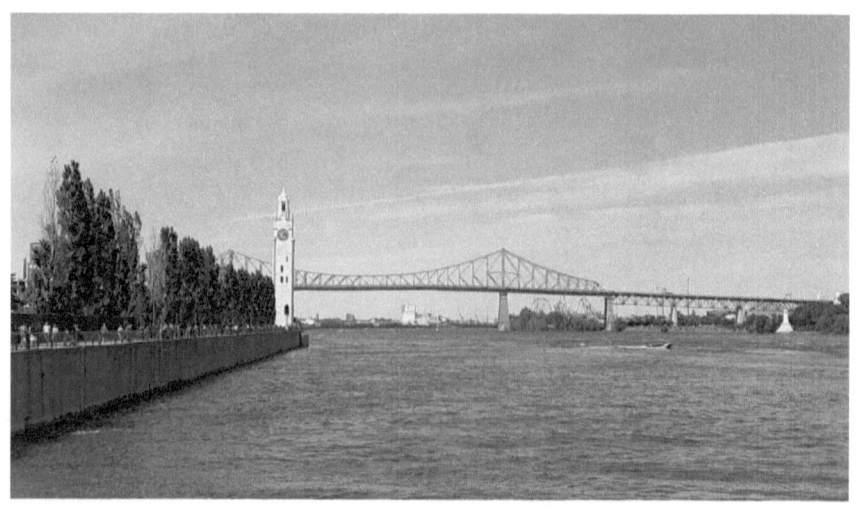

MONTREAL Photos Book 2

CLOCK TOWER 2

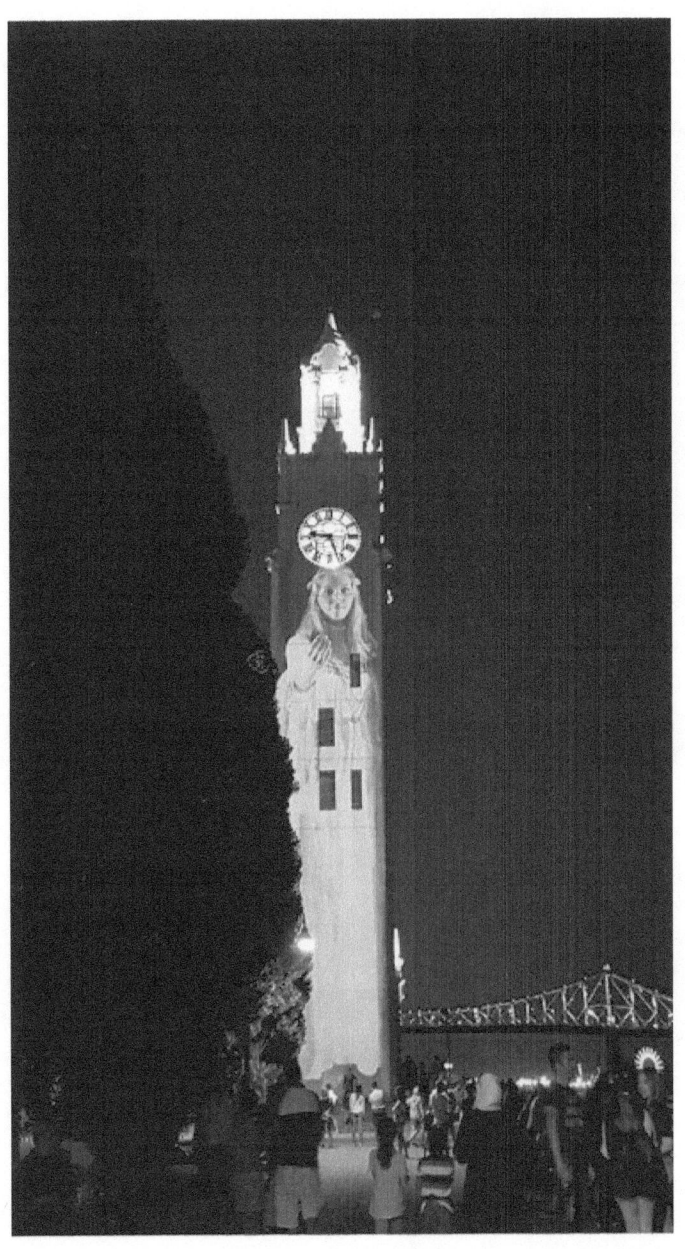

S.E. McKENZIE

L'INTERNATIONAL DES FEUX LOTO-QUEBEC 2018

MONTREAL Photos Book 2

JAZZ FESTIVAL 2018

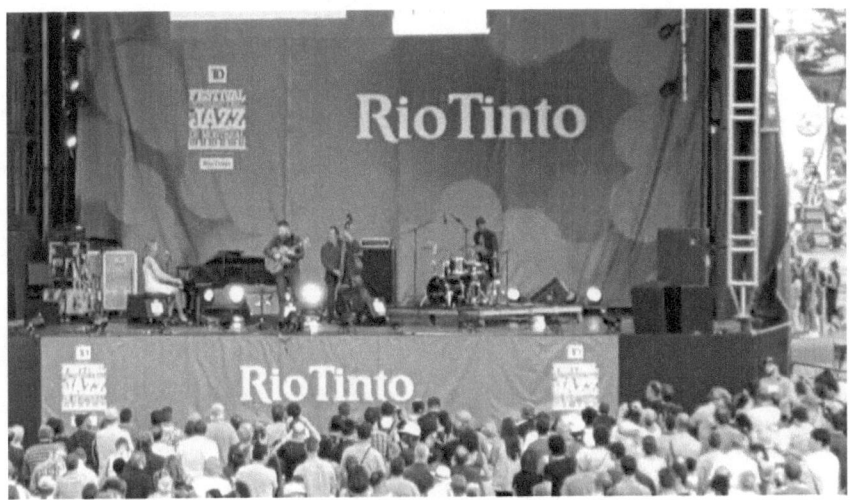

GRAND ORGAN FESTIVAL 1

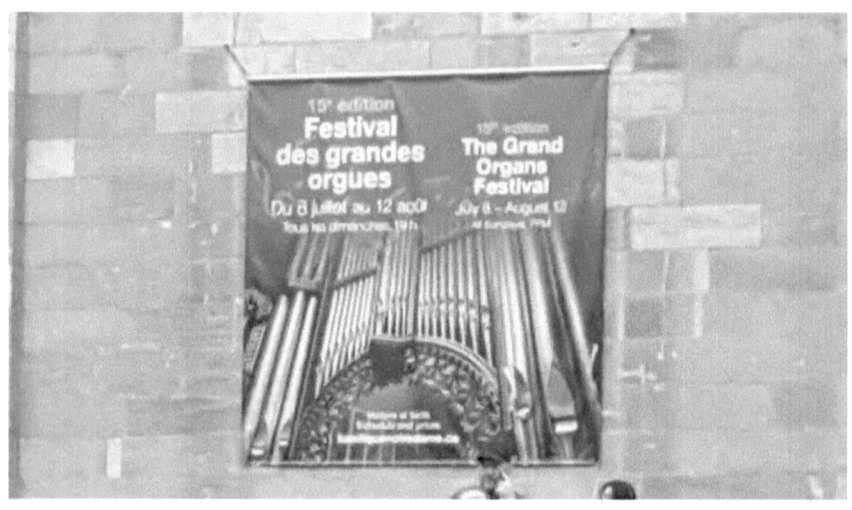

MONTREAL Photos Book 2

GRAND ORGAN FESTIVAL 2

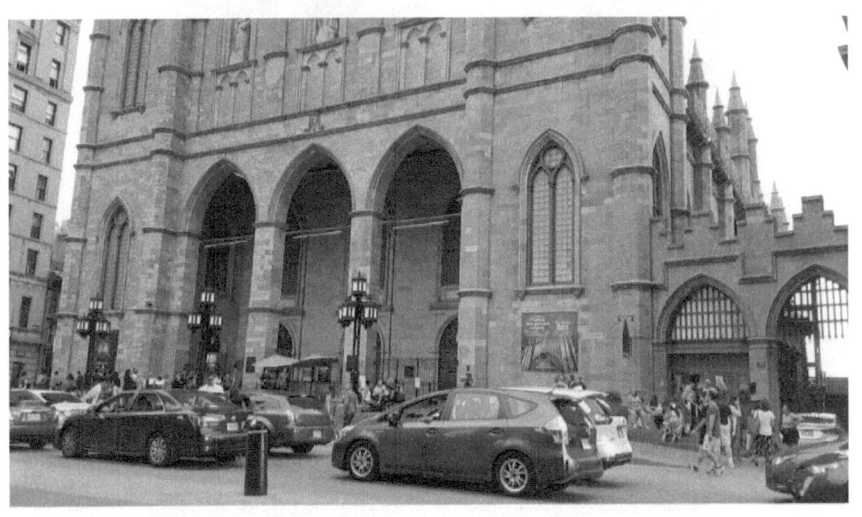

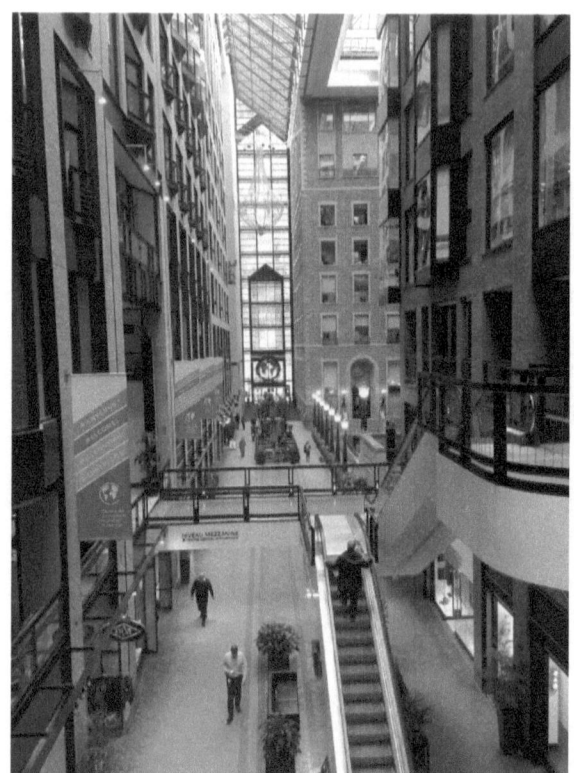

o

MONTREAL Photos Book 2

CRESCENT STREET FESTIVAL 2019-1

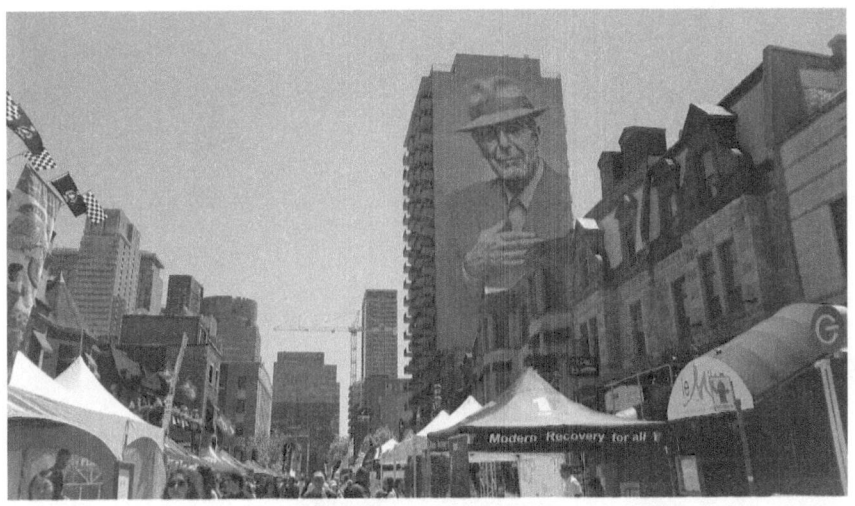

CRESCENT STREET FESTIVAL 2019-2

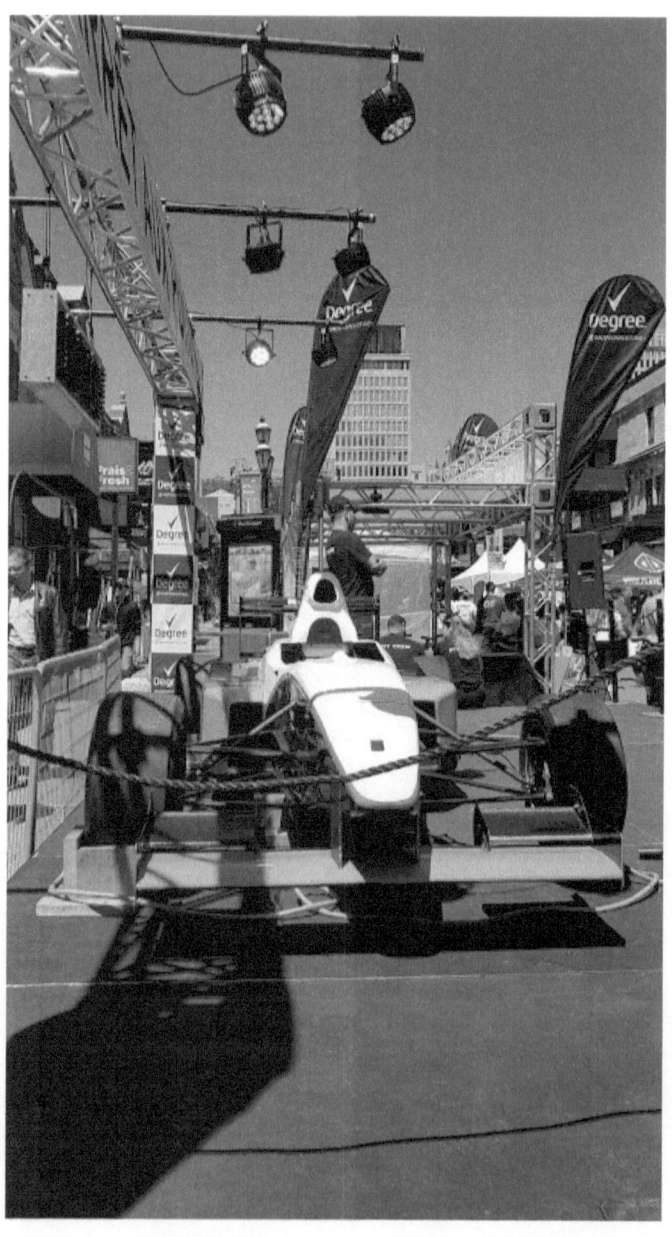

MONTREAL Photos Book 2

CRESCENT STREET FESTIVAL 2019-3

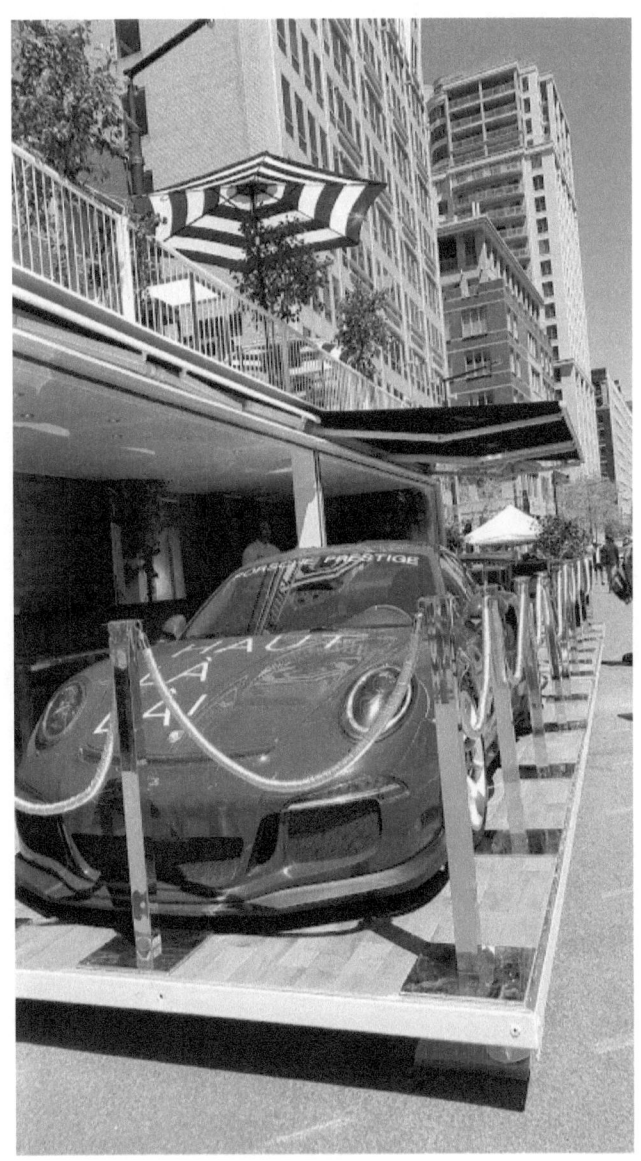

IRISH PARADE

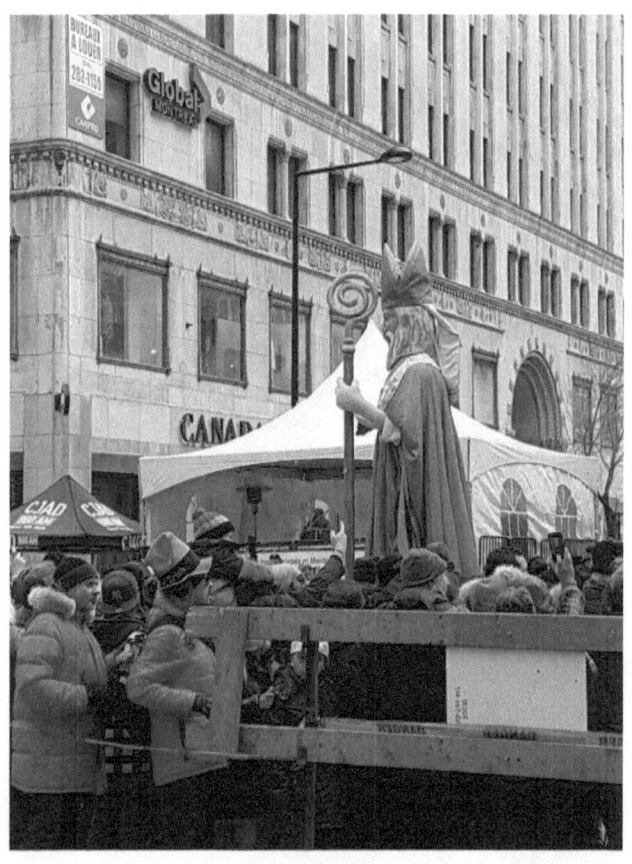

MONTREAL Photos Book 2

NOTRE DAME DE LOURDES CHAPEL-2

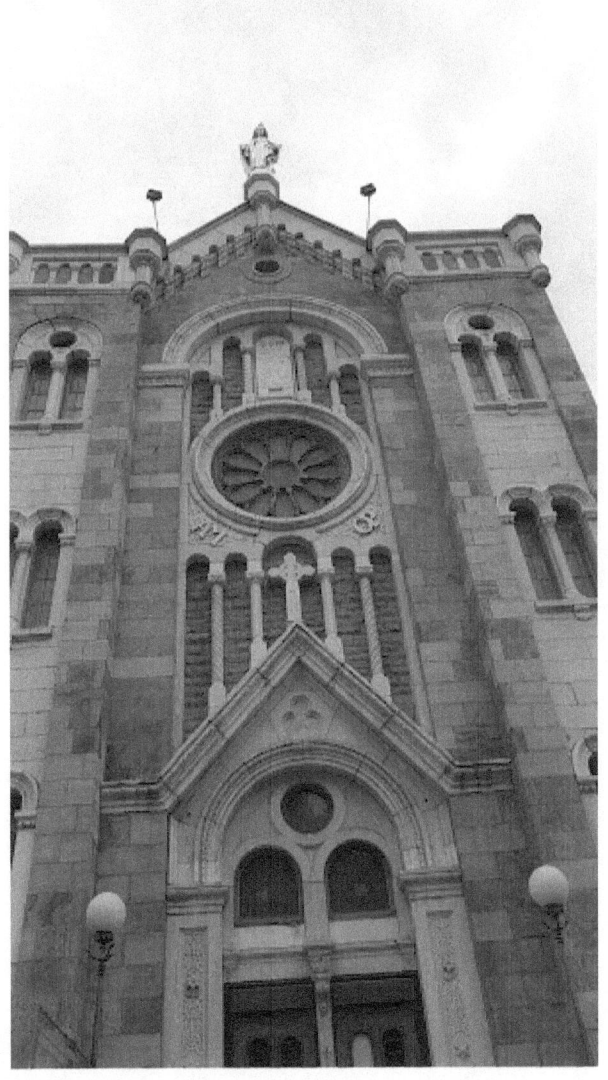

NOTRE DAME DE LOURDES CHAPEL-3

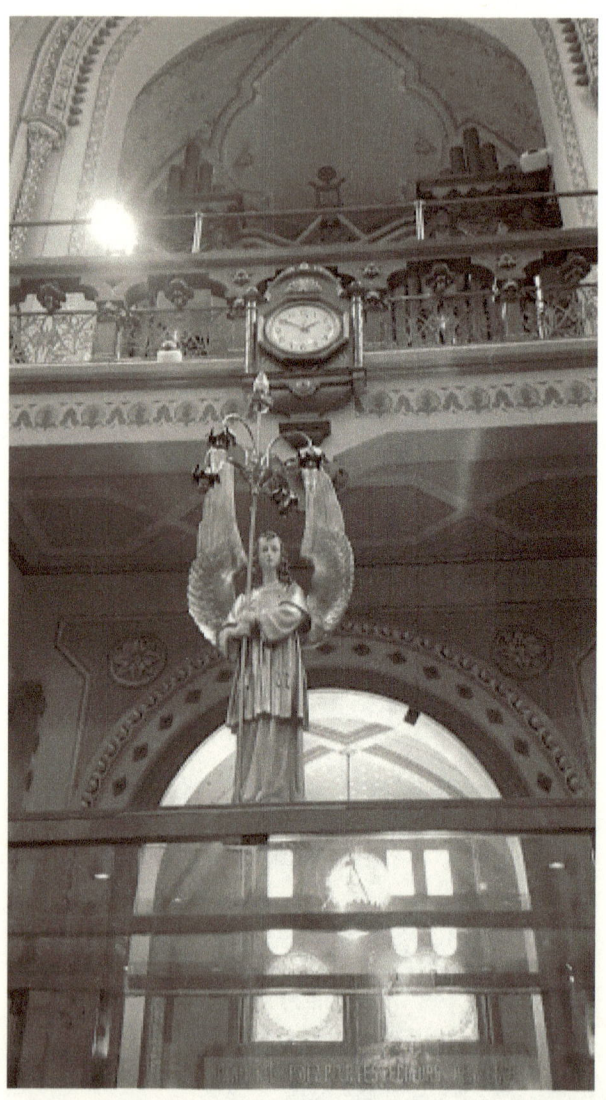

MONTREAL Photos Book 2

VILLAGE-1

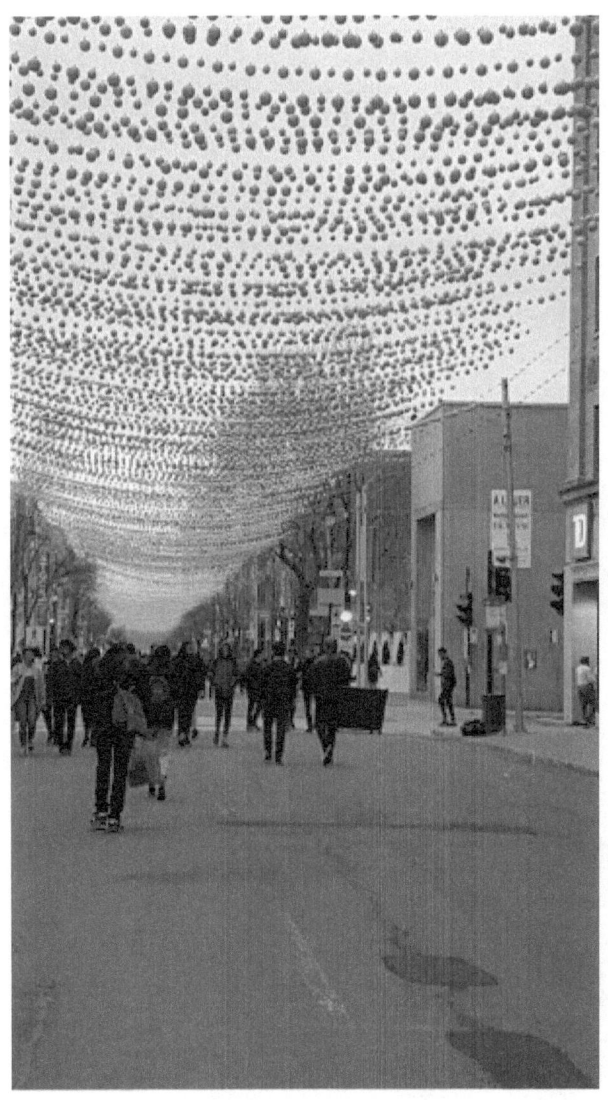

VILLAGE-2

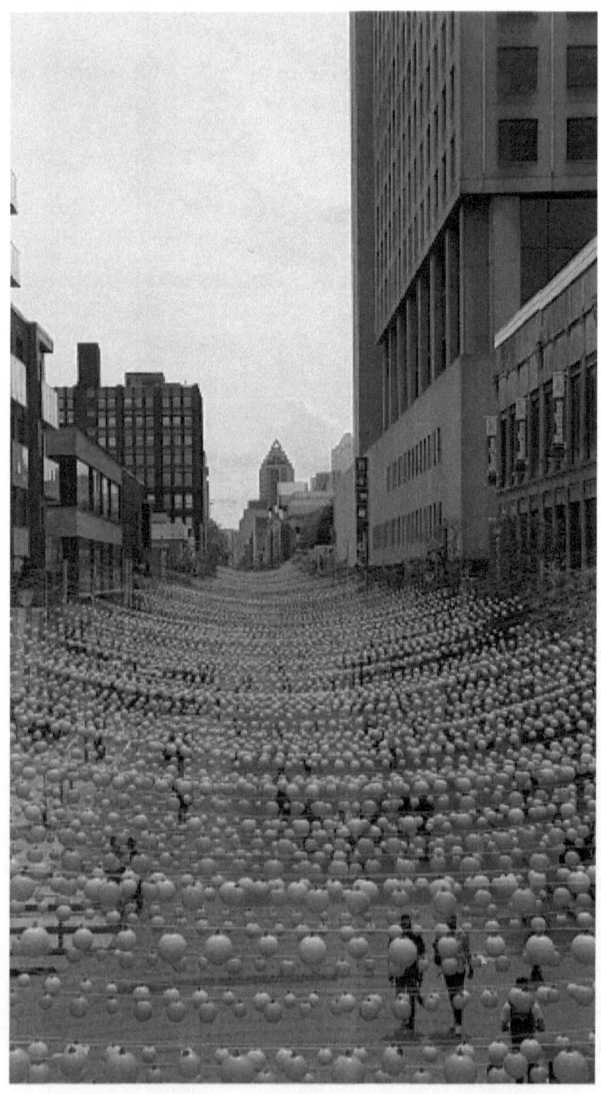

MONTREAL Photos Book 2

JUST FOR LAUGHS PARADE 2018-1

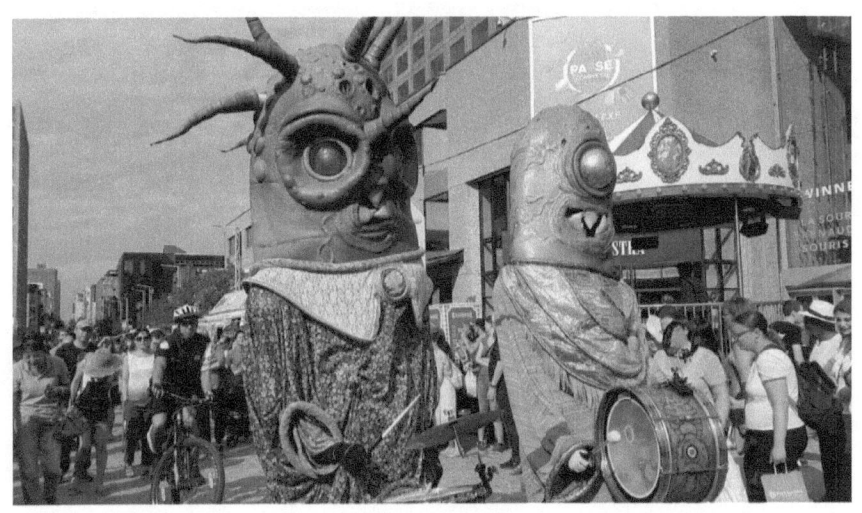

JUST FOR LAUGHS PARADE 2018-2

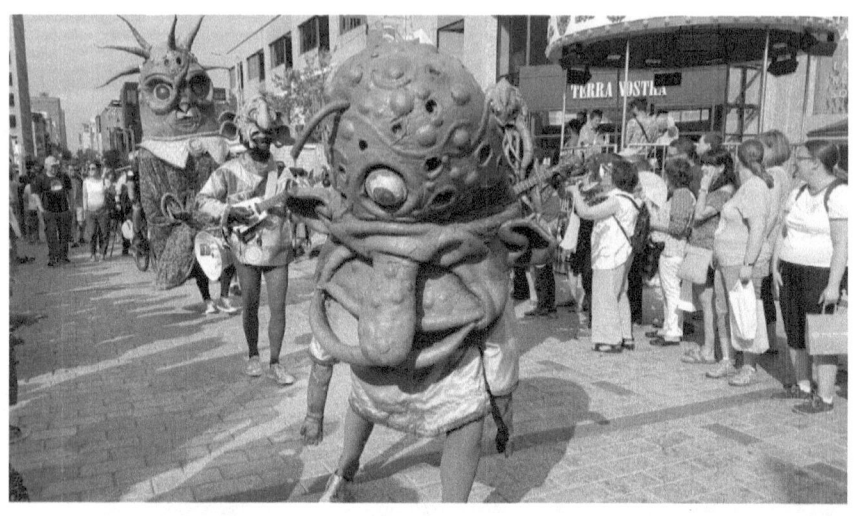

MONTREAL Photos Book 2

JUST FOR LAUGHS 2019-1

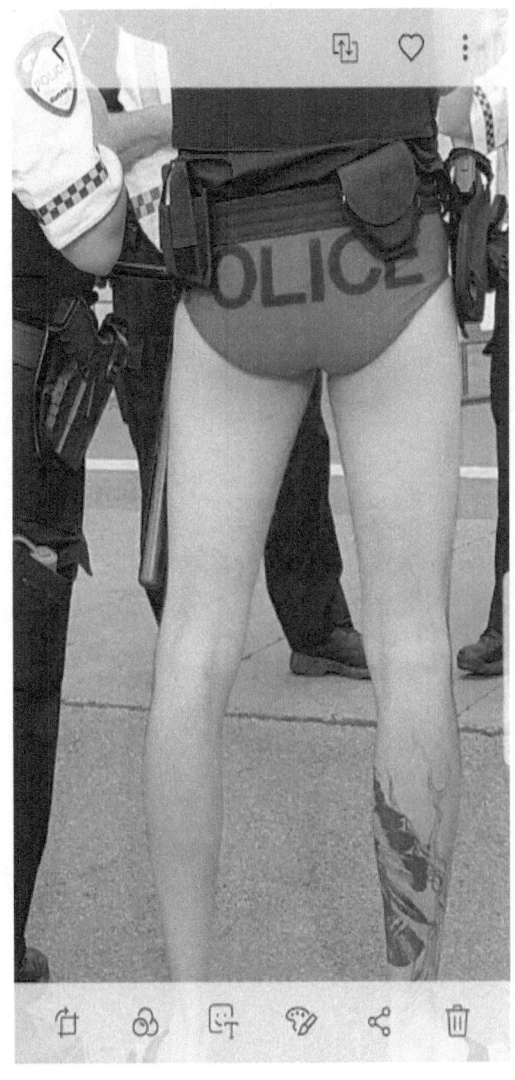

JUST FOR LAUGHS 2019-2

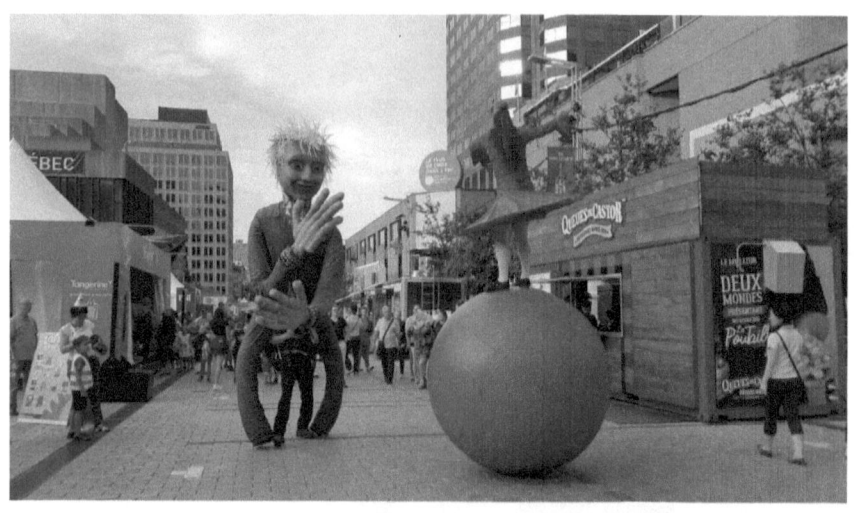

MONTREAL Photos Book 2

JUST FOR LAUGHS 2019-3

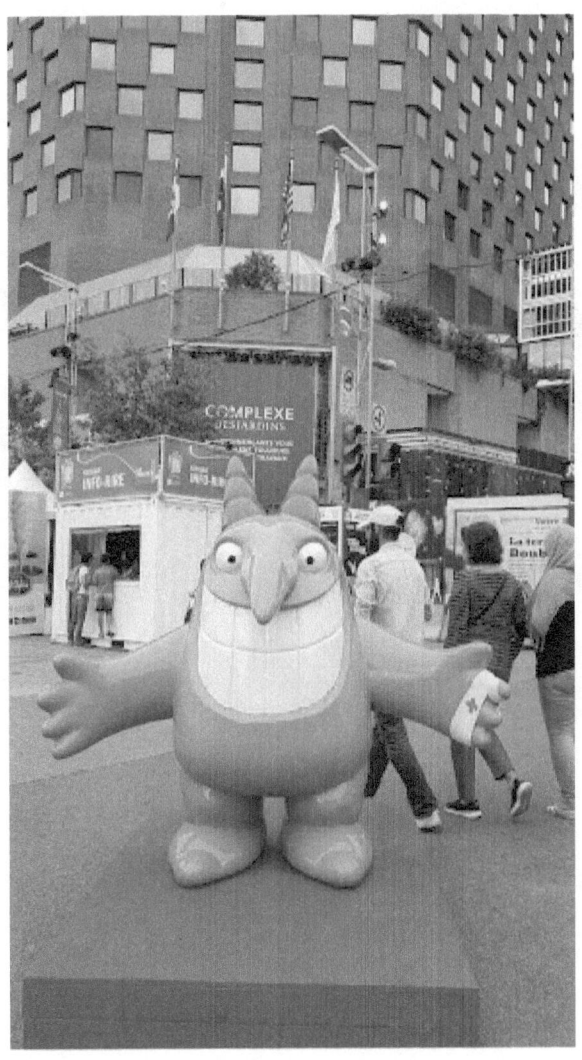

JUST FOR LAUGHS 2019-4

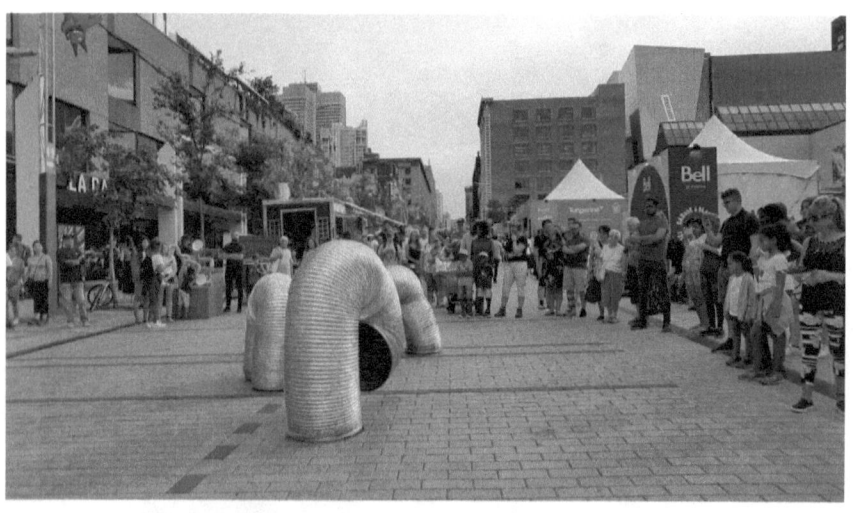

MONTREAL Photos Book 2

JUST FOR LAUGHS 2019-5

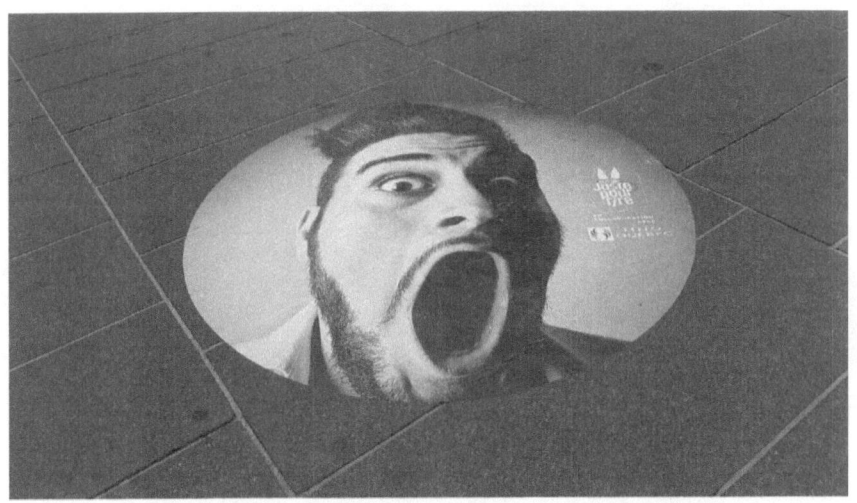

CONSTRUCTION 1

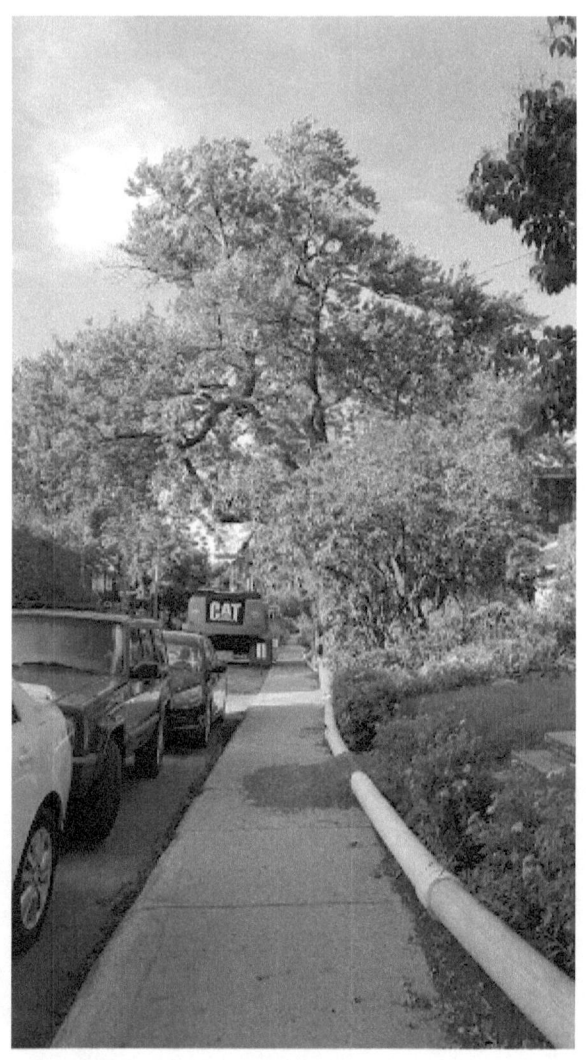

MONTREAL Photos Book 2

CONSTRUCTION 2

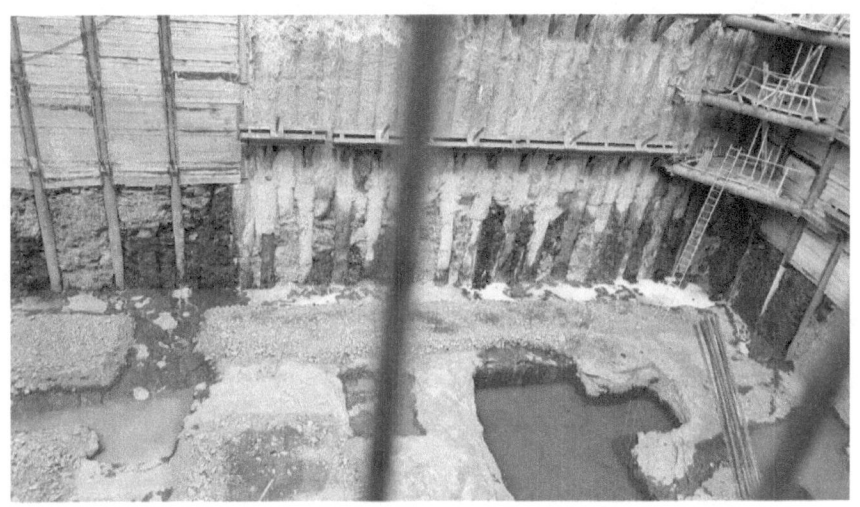

S.E. McKENZIE

GOING BACK IN TIME 1

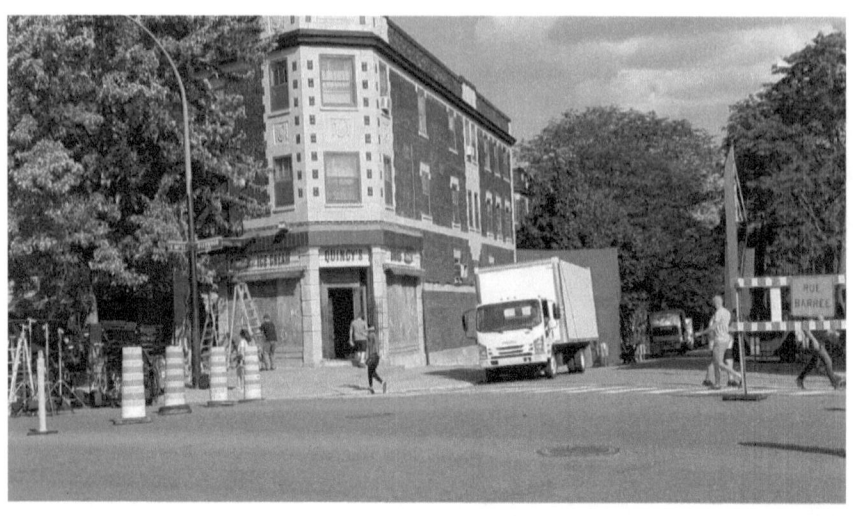

MONTREAL Photos Book 2

GOING BACK IN TIME 2

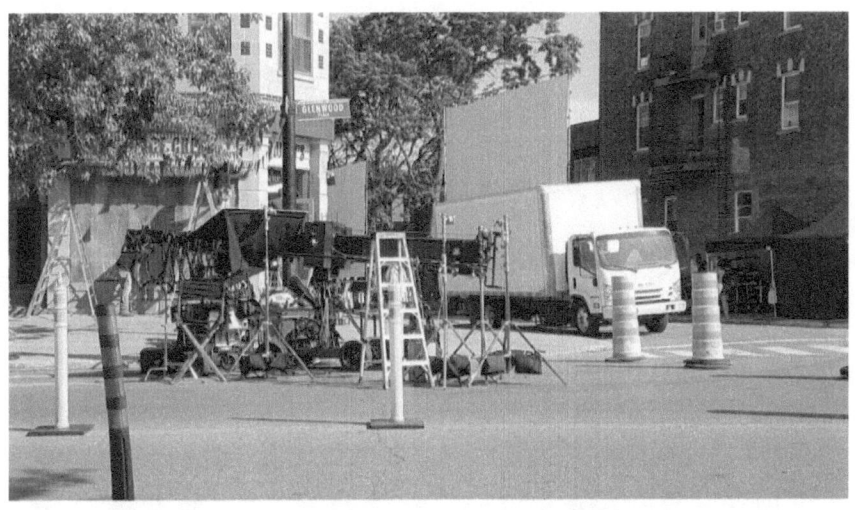

MONTRÉAL COMPLÉTEMENT CIRQUE 2019-3

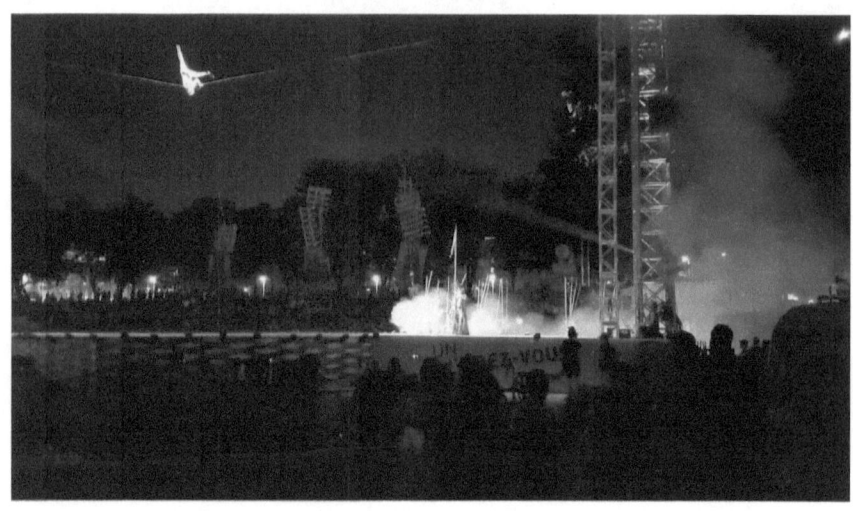

MONTREAL Photos Book 2

OLD PORT 1

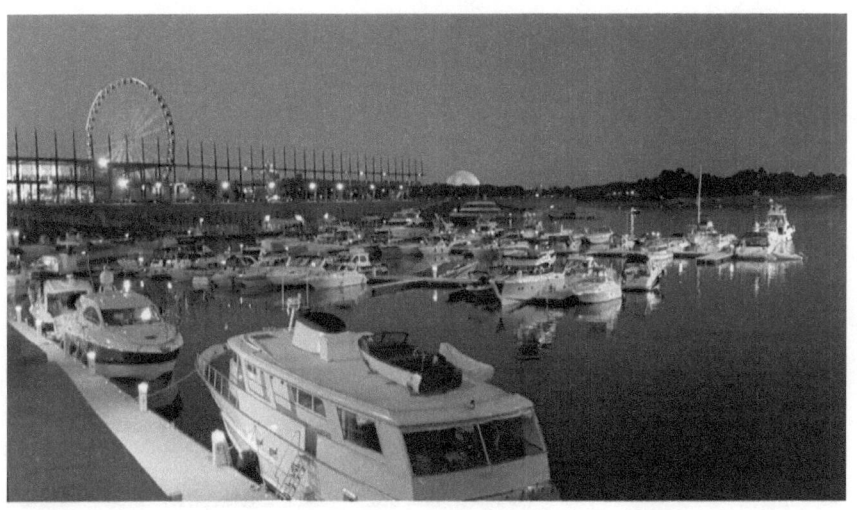

S.E. McKENZIE

OLD PORT 2

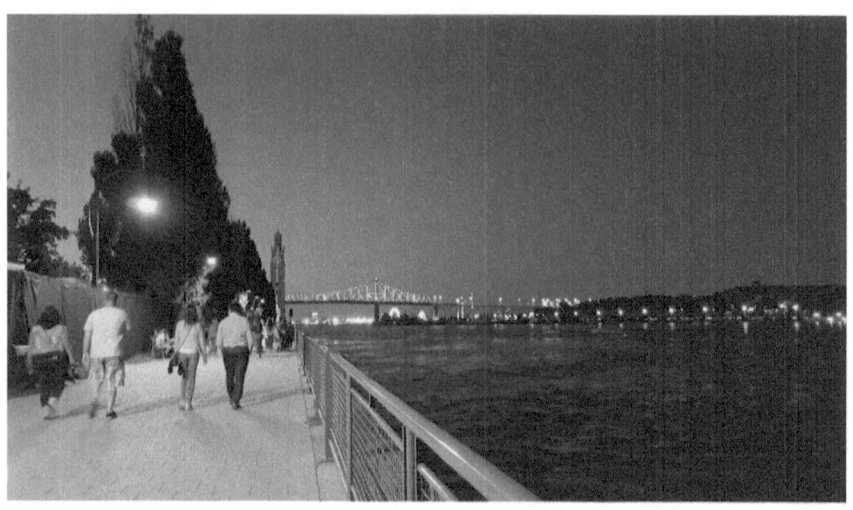

MONTREAL Photos Book 2

OLD PORT 3

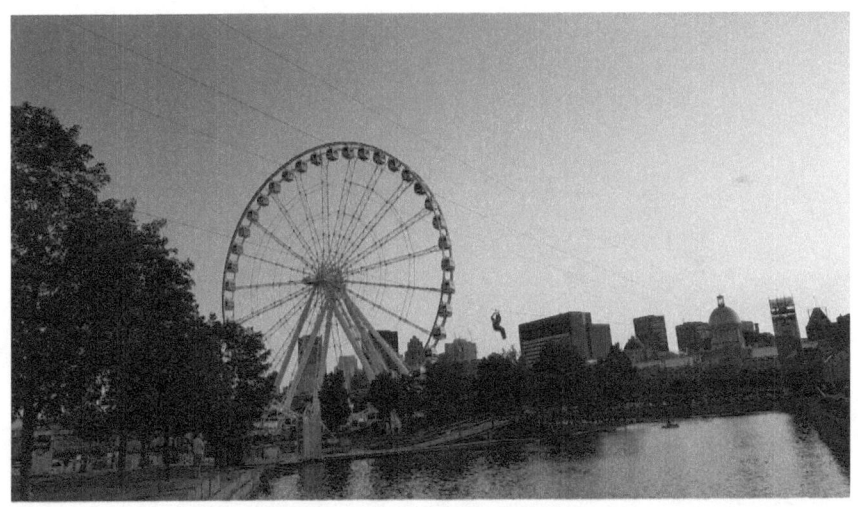

OLD PORT 4

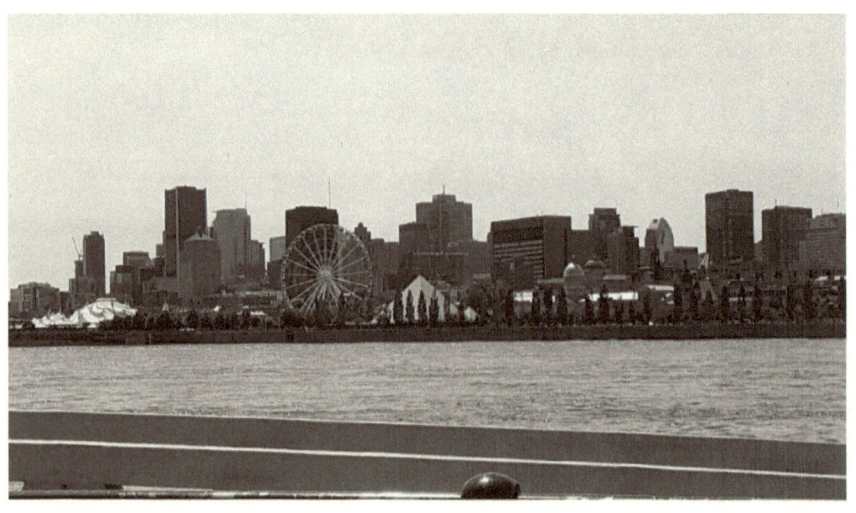

JAZZ FESTIVAL 2019-4

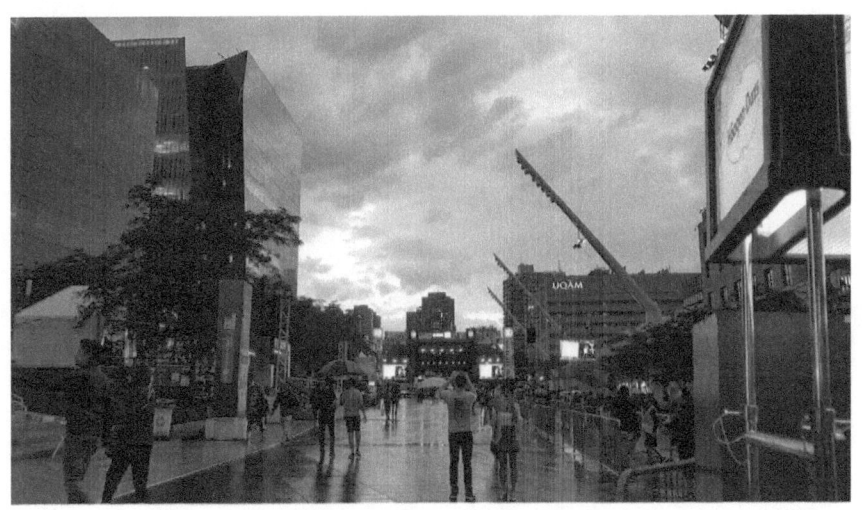

THE END

Produced by S.E. McKenzie Productions
First Print Edition 2019

Copyright © 2019 by S. E. McKenzie
All rights reserved.

Email:
messidartha@aol.com

www.ingramcontent.com/pod-product-compliance
Lightning Source LLC
Chambersburg PA
CBHW030515220526
45464CB00006B/2808